TO
MEEKA · JENNA
KIIRA · MAREE

GOD LOVES YOU ♡

Mike Thaler

2005

HEAVEN AND MIRTH®

Moses

Take Two Tablets and Call Me in the Morning

AND
OTHER BIBLE STORIES TO TICKLE YOUR SOUL

by Mike Thaler
Illustrated by Dennis Adler

Equipping Kids for Life

Dedicated to
Hilma Adler,
in loving memory.
Mike and Dennis

MOSES: TAKE TWO TABLETS AND CALL ME IN THE MORNING
© 2000 by Mike Thaler for text and Dennis Adler for illustrations
FaithKids™ is a registered trademark of Cook Communications Ministries.

HEAVEN AND MIRTH® is a registered trademark of Mike Thaler.

Published in association with the literary agency of Alive Communications, Inc.,
1465 Kelly Johnson Blvd., Suite 320, Colorado Springs, CO 80920.

Edited by Jeannie Harmon
Designed by Clyde Van Cleve

Cook Communications, Colorado Springs, Colorado 80918
Cook Communications, Paris, Ontario
Kingsway Communications, Eastbourne, England

First printing, 2000
Printed in Singapore
04 03 02 01 00   5 4 3 2 1

Thaler, Mike, 1936–
        Moses, take two tablets and call me in the morning: and other Bible stories to tickle your soul
            / by Mike Thaler; illustrated by Dennis Adler. p. cm. – (Heaven and mirth; 3)
        Summary: Five stories based on incidents taken from the Old Testament and written in a humorous way.
        ISBN 0-7814-3262-6
        1. Bible stories, English--O.T. 2. Bible. O.T. Juvenile humor.
        [1. Bible stories –O.T. 2. Bible. O.T. Wit and humor.] I. Adler, Dennis, ill. II. Title. III. Series:
        Thaler, Mike, 1936– Heaven and mirth; 3.
        BS551.2.T45 1999
        221.9'505–dc21

                                                                                                          99–33100
                                                                                                               CIP

Letter from the Author

Taking this opportunity, I would like to share with you how this book came about. Born sixty-two years ago, I have been a secular children's book author most of my life. I was also content to have a fast-food relationship with God from the drive-by window. At the age of sixty, I came into the banquet by inviting Jesus Christ into my heart. Since then my life has been a glorious feast. These stories are part of that celebration.

One night I sat and watched a sincere grandfather trying to read Bible stories to his squirming grandchildren. I asked him, "Aren't there any humorous retellings of Bible stories that are vivid and alive for kids?" He rolled his eyes and said, "This is it." The kids rolled their eyes, too.

This made me sad, for the Bible is the most exciting, valuable, and alive book I know—as is its Author. So I went into my room, with this in mind, and wrote "Noah's Rainbow."

Since then God has anointed me with many stories that fire my imagination and light up my heart. They are stories which, I hope, are filled with the joy, love, and Spirit of the Lord.

Mike Thaler
West Linn 1998

Nuggets from Goldie the miner prophet:
"It's Never Too Late to Eat Right."

Author's Note

I have conscientiously tried to follow each story in word and spirit as found in the Bible. But in some cases, for the sake of storytelling, I have taken minor liberties and added small details, such as saying that Delilah cut off Samson's hair when we know that she actually called in a servant to do it. I pray for your understanding in these instances.

The Israelites in the Desert

This Is the Worst Cruise I've Ever Been On!

THE ISRAELITES were not good travelers, especially in the desert.

"It's too hot," they would complain.

"Roll down the windows," Moses suggested.

"I've got sand in my shoes," they would grumble.

That's how their shoes came to be called *sandals*. Drinking fountains were few and far between. Luckily, public rest rooms were everywhere.

5

As you can guess, food was really scarce. The Israelites all began to complain.

"The travel brochure didn't say anything about starving. We should never have left Egypt. At least we had three square meals a day."*

"God hears all this," said Moses.

"I hear all this," said God.

"Well, if You hear all this," said the Israelites, "let's see a little action."

"All right," said God, **"I know you're hot and hungry. So I'll send air conditioning and some snacks every morning."** And indeed He did. He sent a cool breeze and little white flakes first thing each day.

*Historical Note: They say square meals because they were allowed to eat three bricks a day.

"Man, a* don't know what this stuff is,"
they each said, examining the white flakes.
"It's too big to be dandruff."

"Try it," said Moses. "You'll like it."
They did, and they did.

The Israelites cooked it every way you could imagine.
They had boiled manna, baked manna, barbecued manna.
They had manna teriyaki, manna fricassee, soufflé of manna.
They had manna tacos, manna pizza, and manna-cotti.
They even tried *MANNA HELPER*,
but after a while they began to complain.
"Not manna again!"

So God sent quail
to vary their diet.
He sent *white quail*
that tasted like vanilla
and *brown quail*
that tasted like
chocolate.
He sent *brown and
white mixed quail*,
sort of like a swirl.

*Historical Note:
That's why it came to be called *manna.*

Sometimes the Israelites
would put a quail
between two pieces of manna.
But a little sand always got in,
so they called it a *sandwich*.
Even with all this
abundance from heaven,
the Israelites started to complain again.

"This is worse than airline food!"

"The cholesterol content is not listed."

"Is this stuff kosher?"

Well, the manna continued
to fall in the morning,
and God delivered quail at night,
and the Israelites complained
the rest of the day.

"God, don't You have maybe
a corned beef sandwich
or a little brisket?"

This happened every day,
six days a week, for forty years.

On the seventh day,
God took a rest
from all their complaining.
But the day before,
He gave the Israelites
enough manna for two days.
Of course, they did complain.

"We can't wait till we get to
Miami.
The only thing worse
than *fresh* manna
is *day-old* manna!"

THE END

Nuggets from Goldie, the miner prophet:
"God cares more about your character than your comfort."

For the real story, read Exodus 16.

Moses
Take Two Tablets and Call Me in the Morning

AFTER TRAVELING THREE MONTHS
in the desert, the Israelites
arrived at Mount Sinai.
They pitched their tents,
put in showers, a golf course,
and a Laundromat.

The mountain held a lot of
memories for Moses.
It was the first spot
God had called him
on the hot line.
Since then a lot of water
had flowed over the Egyptians.

Then God spoke to Moses again.
"Moses, it's good to see ya.

"You and these folks mean a lot to Me.
Have them clean up, wash their clothes,
   and relax a little, for in three days
      I'm going to tell them what life's all about."

Then in three days the mountain shook.
   There was lightning and thunder,
      and a large cloud settled over the peak.
      Smoke and fire poured out. Bellowing trumpets blew
      louder and louder. Then God's voice boomed forth!

"I am the Lord, your God.
   I took you out of Egypt and now
  I am going to give you ten rules to live by.
   1. You will have no other gods but Me.
    2. No more bowing down to lawn statues.
     3. Don't use My name in vain . . . or artery.
    4. Slow down . . . think of Me.
    5. Be kind to your mom and dad.
   6. Don't kill anybody.
   7. No hanky panky.
    8. No stealing.
     9. No lying.
      10. And be happy with what you have.
         There'll be another show in two hours."

But the Israelites got scared
and ran into their tents.
Moses climbed up the mountain
and disappeared into the cloud.

**"I hope they didn't get
frightened,"** said God.

"They'll be okay," said Moses.

**"Well, pull up a rock,
I want to talk to you."**

Moses sat down
and God talked to him
for forty days about how to live.
"Could I have something in writing?"
asked Moses, who had had
a little legal training.

"Sure," said God,
and He gave Moses two stone tablets
with the Ten Commandments
written on them.

But in the meantime, the Israelites weren't okay.
They had been so freaked out that they took all their gold

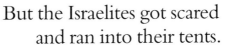

and made a big cow
called Moo-ses,
which they prayed to.
When Moses came down
from the mountain,
he was really miffed.

"You utterly blew it.
I turn my back
for a minute,
and you've already broken
two commandments!"
he shouted, throwing down
the stone tablets.

Then he smashed the gold cow, and
made everyone drink some gold cow's
milk. But Moses loved these people,
so he climbed back up the mountain,
and asked God to forgive them.

"Okay," said God.

"Do you think you could maybe write out
those commandments again?" asked Moses.

"No problem," said God,
   "I've got a Xerox machine."

He quickly gave Moses
   two more stone tablets,
   and they talked
      for another forty days.

When Moses came
   down the mountain this time,
   his face was so bright and shiny
      that everyone
      had to wear sunglasses
      just to talk to him.

THE END

Nuggets from Goldie, the miner prophet:
"When God presents His commandments, He has a very commanding presence."

For the real story, read Exodus 19–34.

Samson
Just a Little Off the Sides

ONCE UPON A TIME
there was a very strong guy
named Samson. When he was a baby,
he could lift camels with a single hand.
He was so strong, even his muscles
had muscles. God had created him
to free the Jews from the bondage of the
Philistines. And when he grew up, they
called him *the Sermonator.*

Now as strong as Samson was, he was not real smart.
Especially when it came to choosing wives.
He picked a Philistine manicurist when he was seventeen.

"Can't you find a nice Jewish girl?" pleaded his father.

"Sorry, Dad, Phyliss Steen is the girl for me."
So with his mom and dad, Samson went courting.

As they approached her house,
 a young lion came roaring across the road.
 Samson got ticked off and ripped it apart
as if it were a fried chicken.
A month later when he went back to marry her,
the lion's carcass was filled with bees
and honey. Samson scooped up some honey
and ate it on the way.

During the wedding feast,
 Samson asked the Philistine guests a riddle.
 He was well-known for his jokes and riddles.

"Why did the lion cross the road?" he smiled.

All the Philistines scratched their heads,
 but could not figure it out. They went to Samson's wife.
 "Get us the answer," they all pleaded.

 Every evening from then on,
she nagged Samson for the answer.
And finally, to get a little peace, he told her,
"To keep the chicken company."

"I don't get it," she said, but she told the Philistines,
and they told Samson, *"To keep the chicken company."*

 "You cheated," pouted Samson,
 who took riddles very seriously, and was not a good loser.

He went out and killed thirty Philistines
and left his wife. But months later he grew lonely,
and went back for her.

"She's remarried and moved away," said her father.

This annoyed Samson even more.
He went out, caught 300 foxes,
tied them together in pairs,
set their tails on fire, and let them loose
in the Philistines' fields,
burning down everything.

Needless to say,
the Philistines didn't take this well.
They sent an army to kill Samson.
When the Jews saw the army,
they went to where Samson was hiding.

"Listen, Samson,
we can't give you the peace prize this year.
You're causing us a lot of trouble."

"Okay," said Samson, "tie me up, and take me
to the Philistines. But as they got close to the army,
Samson snapped his bonds,
picked up the jawbone of a donkey,
and slew a thousand Philistine soldiers.

"There's a good riddle in this somewhere,"
laughed Samson.

For this deed, which the Jews called "JAW,"
they made him their leader.
But he hadn't learned much from his first marriage,
and he fell in love with a Philistine hairstylist
named Delilah.

The Philistine leaders, who were not willing
to forgive and forget, went to Delilah
and offered her silver
for the secret to Samson's strength.

Each night she nagged Samson,
so he told her anything.
One night he said it was his lucky rabbit's foot,
another night he said it was spinach.
But all those proved false.
Delilah nagged on until finally
Samson told the truth, "It's my hair; it's never been cut."

That night when Samson fell asleep, Delilah gave him
a shampoo, a rinse, and clipped off all his hair.
Then she shouted, "Samson, the Philistines are here!"

Samson woke up and weakly felt the top of his head.

"I'm going to stay single from now on," he vowed.
The Philistines fell upon him and put out his eyes.

"Love is blind," joked Samson, who had not lost
his sense of humor. They put him in chains
and set him to work grinding grain.

Then one day the Philistines decided to throw a big party
to celebrate Samson's defeat. They hadn't noticed
that his hair was quickly growing back.
At the height of the party, they brought out Samson
to entertain them. He was sort of a stand-up comic.

He told a few of his favorite riddles,
which got a couple laughs.
Then for his final act, he put his hands
on the central pillars, prayed, and pushed.
This went over so big,
it brought the house down.

THE END

Nuggets from Goldie, the miner prophet:
"When you have more brawn than brain, you wind up being a pushover."

For the real story, read Judges 13–16.

Jonah
The One that Got Away

ONCE UPON A TIME THERE WAS A MAN named Jonah. He was a real whiner, a full-time complainer, not a happy camper. He would grumble to God about everything. It was either too hot or too cold, too dry or too wet. But his biggest complaint was that God forgave everybody.

"No matter what they do, God, You forgive them. Speeding tickets, expired parking meters— how can You run a universe this way? You've got to have order."

"Okay, Jonah," God said, **"go to the wicked city of Nineveh and warn them if they don't get their act together, I'll fold the show."**

"God, it's a long trip and even if I do it,
You'll just forgive them."

"Go, Jonah, go!"

Jonah agreed, but instead of going to Nineveh,
he went the other way.
He got on a boat and sailed toward Tarshish.
Three days out, the sea got choppy.

"Why didn't I take the bus?"
complained Jonah, who was quite green.
The waves swelled into hills.
"It's my fault," Jonah told the crew.
"God is mad at me."

Then the hills rose into mountains
and the little boat fought to stay afloat.

"Throw me into the sea," cried Jonah,
"and the storm will stop."

"No," said the crew, "that isn't the way we treat
our first-class passengers."

"I'm a second-class passenger," said Jonah,
checking his ticket.

"Oh," said the crew, and they threw him into the sea.
He was swallowed by a fabulous fish.

"Boy, it's dark in here," bellyached Jonah.
"And it really smells fishy.
The floor's wet. I'll catch a cold.
And, there are no chairs."

Then Jonah prayed to God,
"Dear God in heaven,
I have just one wish,
get me out of this stinky fish."
God had pity on Jonah
and had the fish burp him
out on a beach.

"What kind of beach is this?
There's no boardwalk,
there's no lifeguard, and besides,
I'm all out of suntan lotion."

"Go to Nineveh and warn them," said God.

"Okay, okay, but it won't do any good."

So Jonah went to the wicked city of Nineveh
and told them, "In forty days God is going to destroy
your entire city. Fire, sword, the whole works."
And because he was such a sincere complainer,
all the Ninevites believed him. They repented
from their wicked ways, they put on sackcloth and ashes,

and they all fasted—everyone from the cop on the beat
to the king on the throne.
And when God saw their repentance,
He forgave them and didn't send destruction.

"I told You You wouldn't do it,"
Jonah wailed to God.
"They deserved it. They were jaywalking,
spitting on the sidewalk,
and double-parking.
You should have destroyed them—
fire, sword, boils, the whole thing.
I'm leaving this city. And besides,
with everyone fasting, you can't get
a decent meal around here anyway."

So Jonah left Nineveh
and sat on top of a mountain.
"Boy, this point is sharp,"
he complained. "It's very hot.
I should have stayed in the fish,
at least it was cool."

God took pity on Jonah
and shaded him with a vine.
"Thanks God, You got maybe
a pair of sunglasses and a visor?"

Then God sent a worm,
and the vine withered and died,
and Jonah really complained.
"God, You killed my vine.
Where's Your heart?"

**"Jonah, you wanted Me to kill
thousands of men, women, and children,
and you gripe about a little vine?"**

"It was a gripe vine, and besides,
I'm into ecology," said Jonah. So he stayed
on the top of the mountain, which
came to be called Holyword and Vine.
He also started a SAVE THE VINE SOCIETY,
and wrote many letters to senators and congressmen
complaining about the treatment of vines and bushes.

P.S. And somewhere at the bottom of the sea,
there's an old fish telling his grandchildren
about the big man that got away.

THE END

Nuggets from Goldie, the miner prophet:
"When you don't follow God's wishes, you may wind up in stinky fishes."

For the real story, read Jonah 1–4.

27

28

Methuselah
A Very Senior Senior

METHUSELAH WAS A SENIOR CITIZEN
most of his life. That's because he lived to be 969 years old.
He practically supported the birthday candle industry.
The local bakery also loved him.
They could count on selling
at least one cake a year.
The Social Security office hated him.
He practically put them out of business.
But everyone else loved him.
Especially his son Lamech,
who was born when Methuselah
was 187 years old.

Methuselah was a great dad.
He coached Little League.

He hit grounders with his cane,
and ran bases with his walker.
He and Lamech also went camping together.
They would have gone fishing, too,
but they lived in the desert.

When asked the secret of his long life, he'd
wink and say, "Just keep breathin'!"

Methuselah saw a lot of changes
in his 969 years. He saw sandals go
from one strap to two.
He saw camels go from one hump
to two. But he never could quite
get used to the newfangled
invention called *fire*.
That was probably due
to his very lengthy beard.
It grew for 900 years
and was about
that many feet long.

Besides flammability,
his beard had other drawbacks.
It got caught in revolving doors,
people dried their hands on it,
and kids used it for a jump rope.

SAND FISHING

But Methuselah was a good sport.
He took it all on the chin,
even when they used it for a hammock.
He'd just stand there and smile
till they woke up.
Having it had good points, too.
He could wear the same tie
and socks every day.
And he could sleep without a blanket
every night.
People also assumed
that he was very wise.
And all he had to do was nod and grin.
So all in all, Methuselah had a pretty good life—
and an enormous photo album.
But, if you meet him in heaven and he starts to show you
pictures of his grandkids. . . run.

THE END

Nuggets from Goldie, the miner prophet:
"With God's help, you can get into the Guinness Book of Records.*"*

For the real story, read Genesis 5:25–27.

HEAVEN AND MIRTH®

Moses

Take Two Tablets and Call Me in the Morning

Age: 6 and up
Life Issue: Learning to trust God no matter what the circumstances.
Spiritual Building Block: Trust

Learning Styles

Help your child learn about trust in the following ways:

Sight: View a story video or read stories from a Bible storybook that recount times when people had to rely on God. Some examples are Daniel in the Lion's den, Queen Esther, Elijah and the prophets of Baal, and Jonah. How did these people know that they could trust God? How do we know that we can trust God?

Sound: When you hear an emergency vehicle siren, discuss with your child the different vehicles that use a siren. It usually means that help is on the way to someone in need. How do we know this? Can we believe that when we have a fire or are in an accident, someone will come and help us? Why?

Touch: Take two puzzles the difficulty level appropriate to your child's age. Place the pieces of one puzzle on the end of a table with the box in plain view. A picture of the completed puzzle should be on the cover. Place the pieces of the other puzzle at the opposite end of the table with no box in view. Which puzzle is easier to assemble? Why? Does the picture make it easier? What if you didn't know for sure if the puzzle was the same picture as the one shown on the box? Do we trust the picture on the box is correct?

Adapted from *Wisdom Life Skills* by Jim Weidmann and Kurt Bruner,
published by Chariot Victor Publishing, page 101.